Spicy ground pork udon

SERVES 2

Quick and easy with no heavy prep
required, as everything just gets thrown
straight into the wok, these spicy
noodles are a simple mid-week winner.

YOU WILL NEED

1tbsp vegetable oil
350g minced pork
1tbsp minced garlic
1tbsp minced ginger
2tbsp doubanjiang (fermented
chilli bean paste)
2tbsp honey
1tbsp white rice vinegar
1tbsp light soy sauce
2tsp dark soy sauce
2tsp chicken powder
or bouillon powder
3 spring onions, roughly
chopped into 5cm lengths
150g bok choy, cut into bite-sized pieces
300g straight-to-wok udon noodles
1tbsp Chinese chilli oil

HOW TO DO IT

1 Place a wok over a medium-high heat,
add the oil and then the pork and fry
for 2-3 mins or until slightly golden
brown. Add the minced garlic and
ginger and continue to fry until fragrant.

2 Stir through the doubanjiang, along
with the honey, vinegar, light and
dark soy sauces, chicken powder and
250ml water, and bring to a boil.

3 Once all of the ingredients are well
combined and hot, turn down to
a simmer and add the spring onions
(scallions) and bok choy.

4 Continue to cook for 2 mins, then
add the noodles and chilli oil and
gently toss to combine the ingredients.
Transfer to serving bowls and enjoy.

ver

Fry

atest Recipes

This is a Parragon Book
This edition published in 2002

Parragon
Queen Street House
4 Queen Street
Bath BA1 1HE, UK

ISBN: 0-75259-292-0

Printed in China

NOTE

This book uses metric and imperial measurements. Follow the same
units of measurement throughout; do not mix metric and imperial.
All spoon measurements are level: teaspoons are assumed to be 5 ml,
and tablespoons are assumed to be 15 ml. Unless otherwise stated,
milk is assumed to be full fat, eggs and individual vegetables such as
potatoes are medium, and pepper is freshly ground black pepper.

The times given for each recipe are an approximate guide only because the
preparation times may differ according to the techniques used by different
people and the cooking times may vary as a result of the type of oven used.
The preparation times include the marinating times, where appropriate.

Recipes using raw or very lightly cooked eggs should be
avoided by infants, the elderly, pregnant women, convalescents,
and anyone suffering from an illness.

C O N T E N T S

INTRODUCTION

Stir-frying is an integral part of Asian and Far Eastern cuisine. It is a light, healthy and very versatile way of cooking. Because stir-fried food is cooked so swiftly, it retains much of its goodness, and has a fresh taste, texture and colour which appeals to the palate and the eye. If you have a wok – or large frying pan – and a spatula for stirring, a whole range of wonderful, easy-to-cook dishes are open to you.

Stir-frying originated in China where it is called *Ch'au*. One or more ingredients are sliced thinly and evenly and cooked in a little oil. The food is stirred all the time with bamboo chopsticks or a spatula. Seasonings and sauces are added towards the end of cooking.

Cooking in a wok

The wok is an ancient Chinese invention for stir-frying. The name comes from the Cantonese for 'cooking vessel'. It is a large, shallow, curved metal bowl, with either a single long wooden handle or two small handles on opposite sides. The most appropriate size of wok for cooking family meals is 30–35 cm/ 12–14 inches in diameter.

   Heat rises around the curved sides of the wok, creating a large, hot cooking surface. Its convex shape means that food can be vigorously tossed around, but always kept in contact with the hot metal – this is the basis of stir-frying.

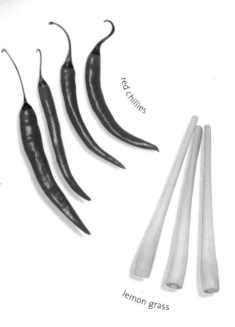

red chillies

lemon grass

Above: Cooking fresh vegetables lightly using small amounts of oil preserves their valuable nutrients, and keeps fat to a minimum.

Different styles

There are different types of stir-frying. *Liu* is wet-frying and stirring the food gently. A cornflour and stock mixture is added with sugar, vinegar and soy sauce at the end of cooking to form a delicious, thick coating sauce.

Pao, or 'explosion', requires foods to be fried at the highest heat, shortly and sharply for about 1 minute. Foods cooked in this way are usually marinated for at least 1 hour beforehand for fuller flavour and tenderness.

Stir-frying is often done in stages. This allows foods which have different cooking times to be stir-fried and removed and then returned to the wok later on as part of the finished dish.

beansprouts

baby corn cobs

pak choi

broccoli

prawn fu yong

hoisin sauce

STORE-CUPBOARD

root ginger

corn oil

mushrooms

Bean sauces

Yellow and black bean sauces are available in the Chinese cooking area of most large supermarkets. Buy a chunky black bean sauce for the best texture and flavour.

Beansprouts

Beansprouts are sprouting mung beans. They should be cooked very lightly to retain their crispness.

Bamboo shoots

Bamboo shoots are added for their crunch, and are a good complement to meat.

Cashew nuts

Cashews add a creamy, rich taste to stir-fries. Always use unsalted nuts, as they are often combined with salty soy sauce.

Chinese five-spice powder

This is a mixture of star anise, fennel, cloves, cinnamon and Szechuan pepper. It adds delicious flavour to beef or pork dishes.

Chinese leaves

Chinese leaves have a lighter, sweeter flavour than white or green cabbage.

Cornflour

Cornflour paste is used to thicken stir-fry sauces. To make it, mix 1 part cornflour with 1.5 parts cold water.

Garlic

Used whole, crushed, sliced or chopped, garlic adds rich flavour to stir-fry cooking oil. It is sometimes removed from the wok before the rest of the ingredients are cooked.

Ginger

Fresh ginger, the root of a plant from Southeast Asia, has a warm, spicy flavour.

Hoisin sauce

This dark brown to reddish sauce is made from soya beans, garlic, chilli and a mixture of spices. It is used frequently in Chinese cookery, and as a dipping sauce.

Mangetouts

Whole, flat, immature pea pods, rich in vitamin C, add a sweet crunchiness to a stir-fry.

garlic

Mushrooms

Many varieties of Chinese mushroom are now available, both dried and fresh. You can find shiitake mushrooms in many supermarkets. Use open-cap mushrooms as an alternative, if you prefer.

Noodles

The most commonly used noodles for stir-fries are thin egg noodles, made from wheat flour, water and egg. Both egg and rice noodles are available fresh and dried, and need very little cooking.

Oils

Groundnut or corn oil are the best oils for stir-frying. They have a high smoking point and mild flavour, so will not burn or taint the food.

Oyster sauce

Oyster sauce is made from oysters cooked in brine and soy sauce and puréed. It will keep for months if stored in a refrigerator.

Rice wine

Use rice wine instead of sherry for an authentic Oriental flavour. Chinese rice wine is made from glutinous rice and is also known as yellow wine because of its golden colour. The best variety, from south eastern China, is called *Shao Hsing* or *Shaoxing*.

Sesame seeds

Toasted sesame seeds are a classic crunchy garnish for many stir-fries.

Soy sauce

Dark and light soy sauces, made from soya beans, are used to season dishes. Light soy sauce is saltier than the dark version.

Spring onions

Spring onions are useful in stir-fries for their mild flavour and crunchy texture.

Szechuan peppercorns

Known as *farchiew*, these wild reddish brown peppercorns from the Szechuan region of China add an aromatic flavour to a dish.

Tofu

Tofu is produced from the soya bean. The cake variety is frequently used in vegetarian stir-fries for its texture, and will absorb the juices and flavours of the other vegetables in the dish. You can buy ready-marinated tofu from most supermarkets.

Water chestnuts

Chinese water chestnuts, or *pi tsi*, are added to stir-fry recipes for their crunchy texture. Today they are grown in China, the East Indies and Japan, and are sliced and canned for export.

spring onions

cashew nuts

chinese cabbage

egg noodles

The one essential piece of equipment for cooking stir-fries is a wok. A large frying pan will perform the same task, but not quite as efficiently.

vegetable knife

wooden spoon

EQUIPMENT

When you are cooking in a wok, several pieces of extra equipment will help you use it to its full potential. Many boxed wok sets contain the following tools as standard.

Collar

One of the most important wok accessories, especially if you have an electric hob, is a metal crown with angled sides which aids heat convection from the cooking ring up the sides of the wok. This heats the wok surface more evenly, rather than just in the centre above the heat source. With or without a collar, on a gas hob you can simply turn the flame up to its highest setting so it laps up the sides of the wok.

Long-handled spatula

A strong, long-handled spatula or paddle is useful for keeping food moving around the wok while it is cooking. Stirring the food helps it to cook evenly. Try to find a spatula with a wooden handle, which will prevent the heat from reaching your hand while stirring.

Shallow wire-mesh basket

Although mainly used for stir-frying, the wok can also be used for deep-frying. A wire-mesh basket is handy for lifting food in and out of the hot oil safely.

Bamboo basket

A wok with a lid can be used as a steamer, and a bamboo basket acts as a steaming trivet. The basket sits in the base of the wok and holds the food clear of the hot water during cooking.

Lid

The lid to a wok is domed, and fits snugly inside the pan to contain the heat during steaming.

chopping boards

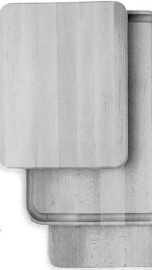

Below and right: Invest in a few sharp knives, a good chopping board and some basic wok accessories to make stir-frying quick and easy.

cook's knife

spatula

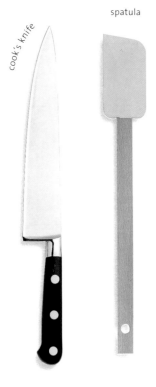

bamboo basket

CHICKEN WITH CASHEW NUTS

>Serves 4 >Preparation time: 30 minutes >Cooking time: 15 minutes

INGREDIENTS

300 g/10½ oz boneless, skinless chicken breasts

1 tbsp cornflour

1 tsp sesame oil

1 tbsp hoisin sauce

1 tsp light soy sauce

3 garlic cloves, crushed

2 tbsp vegetable oil

75 g/2¾ oz unsalted cashew nuts

25 g/1 oz mangetouts

1 celery stick, sliced

1 onion, cut into eight pieces

55 g/2 oz beansprouts

1 red pepper, deseeded and diced

SAUCE

2 tsp cornflour

2 tbsp hoisin sauce

200 ml/7 fl oz chicken stock

METHOD

1 Trim any fat from the chicken breasts and cut the meat into thin strips. Place the chicken in a large mixing bowl. Sprinkle with the cornflour and toss to coat the chicken strips in it, shaking off any excess. Mix together the sesame oil, hoisin sauce, soy sauce and one garlic clove. Pour this mixture over the chicken, turning to coat thoroughly. Leave to marinate for 20 minutes.

2 Heat half of the vegetable oil in a preheated wok or large frying pan. Add the cashew nuts and stir-fry for 1 minute, until browned. Add the mangetouts, celery, the remaining garlic, the onion, beansprouts and red pepper and cook, stirring occasionally, for 2–3 minutes. Remove the vegetables from the wok with a slotted spoon, set aside and keep warm.

3 Heat the remaining oil in the wok. Remove the chicken from the marinade and stir-fry for 3–4 minutes. Return the vegetables to the wok.

4 To make the sauce, mix the cornflour, hoisin sauce and chicken stock together and pour into the wok. Bring to the boil, stirring, until thickened and clear. Serve hot on warmed serving plates.

CHICKEN CHOW MEIN

›Serves 4 ›Preparation time: 5 minutes ›Cooking time: 10–15 minutes

INGREDIENTS

250-g/9-oz packet medium egg noodles

2 tbsp sunflower oil

275 g/9½ oz cooked chicken breasts, shredded

1 clove garlic, finely chopped

1 red pepper, deseeded and thinly sliced

100 g/3½ oz shiitake mushrooms, sliced

6 spring onions, sliced

100 g/3½ oz beansprouts

3 tbsp soy sauce

1 tbsp sesame oil

METHOD

1 Place the noodles in a bowl or dish and break them up slightly. Pour over enough boiling water to cover the noodles and set aside.

2 Heat the sunflower oil in a preheated wok or large frying pan. Add the shredded chicken, chopped garlic, pepper slices, mushrooms, spring onions and beansprouts to the wok and stir-fry for about 5 minutes.

3 Drain the noodles thoroughly. Add the noodles to the wok, toss well and stir-fry for a further 5 minutes.

4 Drizzle the soy sauce and sesame oil over the chow mein and toss until well combined.

5 Transfer the chicken chow mein to warmed serving bowls and serve hot.

CHICKEN CHOP SUEY

>Serves 4 >Preparation time: 25 minutes >Cooking time: 15 minutes

INGREDIENTS

4 tbsp light soy sauce

2 tsp light brown sugar

500 g/1 lb 2 oz skinless, boneless chicken breasts

3 tbsp vegetable oil

2 onions, quartered

2 garlic cloves, crushed

350 g/12 oz beansprouts

3 tsp sesame oil

1 tbsp cornflour

3 tbsp water

425 ml/15 fl oz chicken stock

shredded leek, to garnish

METHOD

1 Mix the soy sauce and sugar together, stirring until the sugar has dissolved.

2 Trim any fat from the chicken and cut into thin strips. Place the meat in a shallow dish and spoon the soy mixture over them, turning to coat. Leave in the refrigerator to marinate for 20 minutes.

3 Heat the oil in a wok or large frying pan and stir-fry the chicken for 2–3 minutes, until golden brown. Add the onions and crushed garlic and cook for a further 2 minutes. Add the beansprouts, cook for 4–5 minutes, then add the sesame oil.

4 Mix the cornflour and water to form a smooth paste. Pour the stock into the wok, add the cornflour paste and bring to the boil, stirring, until the sauce is thickened and clear. Serve, garnished with shredded leek.

EGG-FRIED RICE

> Serves 4   > Preparation time: 20 minutes   > Cooking time: 10 minutes

INGREDIENTS

150 g/5½ oz long-grain rice

3 eggs, beaten

2 tbsp vegetable oil

2 garlic cloves, crushed

4 spring onions, chopped

125 g/4½ oz cooked peas

1 tbsp light soy sauce

pinch of salt

shredded spring onion, to garnish

METHOD

1 Cook the rice in a pan of boiling water for 10–12 minutes, until almost cooked, but not soft. Drain well, rinse under cold water and drain again.

2 Place the beaten eggs in a pan and cook over a gentle heat, stirring until softly scrambled.

3 Heat the vegetable oil in a preheated wok or large frying pan, swirling the oil around the base of the wok until it is really hot.

4 Add the crushed garlic, spring onions and peas and sauté, stirring occasionally, for about 1–2 minutes. Stir the rice into the wok, mixing to combine.

5 Add the eggs, light soy sauce and a pinch of salt to the wok and mix thoroughly.

6 Transfer the rice to serving dishes, garnish with the shredded spring onion and serve.

16

FRUITY DUCK STIR-FRY

>Serves 4   >Preparation time: 5 minutes   >Cooking time: 25–30 minutes

INGREDIENTS

4 duck breasts

1 tsp Chinese five-spice powder

1 tbsp cornflour

1 tbsp chilli oil

225 g/8 oz baby onions, peeled

2 cloves garlic, crushed

100 g/3½ oz baby corn cobs

175 g/6 oz canned pineapple chunks

6 spring onions, sliced

100 g/3½ oz beansprouts

2 tbsp plum sauce

METHOD

1 Remove any skin from the duck breasts. Cut the duck into thin slices.

2 Mix the five-spice powder and the cornflour. Toss the duck in the mixture until well coated.

3 Heat the chilli oil in a preheated wok or large frying pan. Stir-fry the duck for 10 minutes, or until just beginning to crisp around the edges. Remove from the wok and set aside.

4 Add the onions and garlic to the wok and stir-fry for 5 minutes, or until softened. Add the baby corn and stir-fry for a further 5 minutes. Add the pineapple, spring onions and beansprouts and stir-fry for 3–4 minutes. Stir in the plum sauce.

5 Return the cooked duck to the wok and toss until well mixed. Transfer to warmed serving dishes and serve hot.

LAMB WITH SATAY SAUCE

>Serves 4   >Preparation time: 40 minutes   >Cooking time: 20 minutes

INGREDIENTS

450 g/1 lb lamb loin fillet

1 tbsp mild curry paste

150 ml/5 fl oz coconut milk

2 cloves garlic, crushed

½ tsp chilli powder

½ tsp cumin

SATAY SAUCE

1 tbsp corn oil

1 onion, diced

6 tbsp crunchy peanut butter

1 tsp tomato purée

1 tsp fresh lime juice

100 ml/3½ fl oz cold water

METHOD

1 Using a sharp knife, thinly slice the lamb and place in a large dish.

2 Mix together the curry paste, coconut milk, garlic, chilli powder and cumin in a bowl. Pour over the lamb, toss well, cover and marinate for 30 minutes.

3 To make the satay sauce, heat the oil in a wok or frying pan, stir-fry the onion for 5 minutes, then reduce the heat and cook for 5 minutes.

4 Stir in the peanut butter, tomato purée, lime juice and water and set aside.

5 Thread the lamb on to wooden skewers, reserving the marinade.

6 Grill the lamb skewers under a hot grill for 6–8 minutes, turning once.

7 Meanwhile, add the reserved marinade to the wok, bring to the boil and cook for 5 minutes. Serve the lamb skewers with the satay sauce.

17

VEGETABLE CHOP SUEY

> Serves 4   > Preparation time: 3 minutes   > Cooking time: 7 minutes

INGREDIENTS

2 tbsp groundnut oil

1 onion, chopped

3 garlic cloves, chopped

1 green pepper, deseeded and diced

1 red pepper, deseeded and diced

75 g/2¾ oz broccoli florets

1 courgette, sliced

25 g/1 oz French beans

1 carrot, cut into matchsticks

100 g/3½ oz beansprouts

2 tsp light brown sugar

2 tbsp light soy sauce

125 ml/4 fl oz vegetable stock

salt and pepper

noodles, to serve

METHOD

1 Heat the oil in a preheated wok or large frying pan until almost smoking. Add the onion and garlic and stir-fry for 30 seconds.

2 Stir in the diced peppers, broccoli, courgette, French beans and carrot and stir-fry for a further 2–3 minutes.

3 Add the beansprouts, light brown sugar, soy sauce and vegetable stock. Season to taste and cook for about 2 minutes.

4 Transfer the vegetables to serving plates and serve hot with noodles.

PORK FRY WITH VEGETABLES

>Serves 4 >Preparation time: 5 minutes >Cooking time: 15 minutes

INGREDIENTS

350 g/12 oz lean pork fillet

2 tbsp vegetable oil

2 garlic cloves, crushed

1-cm/½-inch piece fresh root ginger, cut into slivers

1 carrot, cut into thin strips

1 red pepper, deseeded and diced

1 fennel bulb, sliced

25 g/1 oz water chestnuts, halved

75 g/2¾ oz beansprouts

2 tbsp Chinese rice wine

300 ml/10 fl oz pork or chicken stock

pinch of dark brown sugar

1 tsp cornflour

2 tsp water

METHOD

1 Cut the pork fillet into thin slices. Heat the oil in a preheated wok or large frying pan. Add the garlic, ginger and pork and stir-fry for 1–2 minutes, until the meat is sealed.

2 Add the carrot strips, pepper, fennel and water chestnuts to the wok and stir-fry for about 2–3 minutes.

3 Add the beansprouts and continue stir-frying for 1 minute. Remove the pork and vegetables from the wok and keep warm.

4 Add the Chinese rice wine, pork or chicken stock and sugar to the wok. Blend the cornflour to a smooth paste with the water and stir it into the sauce. Bring to the boil, stirring constantly, until thickened and clear.

5 Return the meat and vegetables to the wok and cook for 1–2 minutes, until heated through and coated with the sauce. Serve hot.

LEMON CHICKEN

>Serves 4   >Preparation time: 5 minutes   >Cooking time: 15 minutes

INGREDIENTS

vegetable oil, for deep-frying

650 g/1 lb 7 oz skinless, boneless chicken, cut into strips

SAUCE

1 tbsp cornflour

6 tbsp cold water

3 tbsp fresh lemon juice

2 tbsp sweet sherry

½ tsp caster sugar

TO GARNISH

lemon slices

shredded spring onion

METHOD

1 Heat the oil for deep-frying in a preheated wok or large frying pan to 180°C/350°F, or until a cube of bread browns in 30 seconds.

2 Reduce the heat and stir-fry the chicken strips for 3–4 minutes, until cooked through.

3 Remove the chicken with a slotted spoon, set aside and keep warm. Drain the hot oil from the wok.

4 To make the sauce, mix the cornflour with 2 tablespoons of the water to form a paste.

5 Pour the lemon juice and remaining water into the wok.

6 Add the sweet sherry and caster sugar and bring to the boil, stirring, until the sugar has completely dissolved.

7 Stir in the cornflour mixture and return to the boil. Reduce the heat and simmer, stirring constantly, for 2–3 minutes, until the sauce is thickened and clear.

8 Transfer the chicken to a warmed serving plate and pour the sauce over the top.

9 Garnish the chicken with the lemon slices and shredded spring onion and serve hot.

OYSTER SAUCE BEEF

›Serves 4 ›Preparation time: 40 minutes ›Cooking time: 5 minutes

INGREDIENTS

300 g/10½ oz beef steak

1 tsp sugar

1 tbsp light soy sauce

1 tsp rice wine or dry sherry

1 tsp cornflour

½ small carrot

55 g/2 oz mangetouts

55 g/2 oz canned bamboo shoots

55 g/2 oz canned straw mushrooms

about 300 ml/10 fl oz vegetable oil

1 spring onion, cut into short sections

2–3 small slices of fresh root ginger

½ tsp salt

2 tbsp oyster sauce

2–3 tbsp vegetable stock or water

METHOD

1 Cut the beef into small, thin slices. Place in a shallow dish with the sugar, soy sauce, wine and cornflour and set aside to marinate for 25–30 minutes.

2 Slice the carrot, mangetouts, bamboo shoots and straw mushrooms into pieces roughly the same size as each other.

3 Heat the oil in a wok or large frying pan and add the beef. Stir-fry for 1 minute, then remove and keep warm.

4 Pour off the oil, leaving about 1 tablespoon in the wok. Add the sliced vegetables with the spring onion and ginger and stir-fry for about 2 minutes. Add the salt, beef, oyster sauce and stock or water. Blend well until heated through and serve.

21

SESAME LAMB STIR-FRY

>Serves 4 >Preparation time: 5 minutes >Cooking time: 10 minutes

INGREDIENTS

450 g/1 lb lean boneless lamb

2 tbsp groundnut oil

2 leeks, sliced

1 carrot, cut into matchsticks

2 garlic cloves, crushed

85 ml/3 fl oz lamb or vegetable stock

2 tsp light brown sugar

1 tbsp dark soy sauce

4½ tsp sesame seeds

METHOD

1 Using a sharp knife, carefully slice the lamb into thin strips.

2 Heat the groundnut oil in a preheated wok or large frying pan until it is really hot.

3 Add the lamb and stir-fry for 2–3 minutes. Remove the lamb from the wok with a slotted spoon and set aside until required.

4 Add the leeks, carrot and garlic to the wok. Stir-fry in the remaining oil for 1–2 minutes.

5 Remove the vegetables from the wok with a slotted spoon and set aside.

6 Drain any remaining oil from the wok. Place the lamb or vegetable stock, light brown sugar and dark soy sauce in the wok and add the lamb. Cook, stirring constantly to coat the lamb, for 2–3 minutes.

7 Sprinkle the sesame seeds over the top, turning the lamb to coat.

8 Spoon the leek, carrot and garlic mixture on to a warmed serving dish and top with the lamb. Serve hot.

PRAWN FU YONG

>Serves 4 >Preparation time: 5 minutes >Cooking time: 10 minutes

INGREDIENTS

2 tbsp vegetable oil

1 carrot, grated

5 eggs, beaten

225 g/8 oz raw prawns, peeled

1 tbsp light soy sauce

pinch of Chinese five-spice powder

2 spring onions, chopped

2 tsp sesame seeds

1 tsp sesame oil

METHOD

1 Heat the vegetable oil in a preheated wok or large frying pan, swirling it around until the oil is really hot.

2 Add the carrot and stir-fry for 1–2 minutes.

3 Push the carrot to one side of the wok and add the beaten eggs. Cook, stirring gently, for 1–2 minutes.

4 Stir the prawns, light soy sauce and five-spice powder into the mixture in the wok. Stir-fry for 2–3 minutes, or until the prawns change colour and the mixture is almost dry.

5 Turn the prawn fu yong out on to a warmed plate and sprinkle the spring onions, sesame seeds and sesame oil on top. Serve hot.

24

SPICY BEEF

> Serves 4   > Preparation time: 1¼ hours   > Cooking time: 10 minutes

INGREDIENTS

225 g/8 oz fillet steak

2 garlic cloves, crushed

1 tsp powdered star anise

1 tbsp dark soy sauce

spring onion tassels, to garnish

SAUCE

2 tbsp vegetable oil

1 bunch spring onions, halved lengthways

1 tbsp dark soy sauce

1 tbsp dry sherry

¼ tsp chilli sauce

150 ml/5 fl oz water

2 tsp cornflour

METHOD

1 Cut the steak into thin strips and place in a shallow dish.

2 Mix together the garlic, star anise and dark soy sauce in a bowl.

3 Pour the sauce mixture over the steak strips, turning them to coat thoroughly. Cover and leave to marinate in the refrigerator for at least 1 hour.

4 To make the sauce, heat the oil in a preheated wok or large frying pan. Reduce the heat and stir-fry the halved spring onions for 1–2 minutes.

5 Remove the spring onions from the wok with a slotted spoon, drain on kitchen paper and set aside until required.

6 Add the beef and its marinade to the wok and stir-fry for 3–4 minutes. Return the spring onions to the wok and add the soy sauce, sherry, chilli sauce and two thirds of the water.

7 Blend the cornflour with the remaining water and stir into the wok. Bring to the boil, stirring, until the sauce thickens and clears.

8 Transfer to a warmed serving dish, garnish with spring onion tassels and serve hot.

SWEET & SOUR NOODLES

>Serves 4   >Preparation time: 10 minutes   >Cooking time: 10 minutes

INGREDIENTS

3 tbsp fish sauce

2 tbsp distilled white vinegar

2 tbsp caster or palm sugar

2 tbsp tomato purée

2 tbsp sunflower oil

3 cloves garlic, crushed

350 g/12 oz rice noodles, soaked in boiling
water for 5 minutes

8 spring onions, sliced

2 carrots, grated

150 g/5½ oz beansprouts

2 eggs, beaten

225 g/8 oz peeled king prawns

50 g/1¼ oz chopped peanuts

1 tsp chilli flakes, to garnish

METHOD

1 Mix together the fish sauce, vinegar, sugar
and tomato purée.

2 Heat the oil in a preheated wok or large
frying pan.

3 Add the crushed garlic to the wok and stir-fry
for 30 seconds.

4 Drain the noodles thoroughly and add them
to the wok together with the fish sauce and
tomato purée mixture. Mix well to combine.

5 Add the sliced spring onions, grated carrot
and beansprouts to the wok and stir-fry for
2–3 minutes.

6 Move the stir-fry mixture to one side of the
wok, add the beaten eggs to the empty part of
the wok and cook until the egg sets. Add the
noodles, prawns and peanuts to the wok and
mix well. Transfer to warmed serving dishes
and garnish with chilli flakes. Serve hot.

STIR-FRIED SALMON WITH LEEKS

›Serves 4 ›Preparation time: 35 minutes ›Cooking time: 15 minutes

INGREDIENTS

450 g/1 lb salmon fillet, skinned

2 tbsp sweet soy sauce

2 tbsp tomato ketchup

1 tsp rice wine vinegar

1 tbsp demerara sugar

1 clove garlic, crushed

4 tbsp corn oil

450 g/1 lb leeks, thinly shredded

finely chopped red chillies, to garnish

METHOD

1 Using a sharp knife, cut the salmon into slices. Place the fish slices in a shallow, non-metallic dish.

2 Mix together the soy sauce, tomato ketchup, rice wine vinegar, sugar and garlic.

3 Pour the mixture over the salmon, toss well and leave to marinate for about 30 minutes.

4 Meanwhile, heat 3 tablespoons of the corn oil in a preheated wok or large frying pan.

5 Add the leeks to the wok and stir-fry over a medium–high heat for about 10 minutes, or until the leeks become crispy and tender.

6 Using a slotted spoon, carefully remove the leeks from the wok and transfer to warmed serving plates.

7 Add the remaining oil to the wok. Add the salmon and the marinade to the wok and cook for 2 minutes.

8 Remove the salmon from the wok and spoon over the leeks, garnish with finely chopped red chillies and serve hot.

BEEF, PEPPERS & LEMON GRASS

>Serves 4   >Preparation time: 5–10 minutes   >Cooking time: 10 minutes

INGREDIENTS

500 g/1 lb 2 oz lean beef fillet

2 tbsp vegetable oil

1 garlic clove, finely chopped

1 lemon grass stalk, finely shredded

2.5-cm/1-inch piece fresh root ginger, finely chopped

1 red pepper, deseeded and thickly sliced

1 green pepper, deseeded and thickly sliced

1 onion, thickly sliced

2 tbsp lime juice

salt and pepper

boiled noodles or rice, to serve

METHOD

1 Cut the beef into long, thin strips, cutting across the grain.

2 Heat the oil in a wok or large frying pan over a high heat. Add the chopped garlic and stir-fry for 1 minute.

3 Add the beef and stir-fry for a further 2–3 minutes until lightly coloured. Stir in the lemon grass and ginger and remove the wok from the heat.

4 Remove the beef from the wok and set aside. Add the sliced red and green peppers and onion to the wok and stir-fry over a high heat for 2–3 minutes until the onions are just turning golden brown and slightly softened.

5 Return the beef to the wok, stir in the lime juice and season to taste with salt and pepper. Serve with noodles or rice.

27

SWEET & SOUR PORK

> Serves 4 > Preparation time: 10 minutes > Cooking time: 20 minutes

INGREDIENTS

150 ml/5 fl oz vegetable oil, for deep-frying

225 g/8 oz pork fillet, cut into 1-cm/½-inch cubes

1 onion, sliced

1 green pepper, deseeded and sliced

225 g/8 oz canned pineapple pieces

1 small carrot, cut into thin strips

25 g/1 oz canned bamboo shoots, drained, rinsed and halved

rice or noodles, to serve

BATTER

125 g/4½ oz plain flour

1 tbsp cornflour

1½ tsp baking powder

1 tbsp vegetable oil

SAUCE

125 g/4½ oz light brown sugar

2 tbsp cornflour

125 ml/4 fl oz white wine vinegar

2 garlic cloves, crushed

4 tbsp tomato purée

6 tbsp pineapple juice

METHOD

1 To make the batter, sift the plain flour into a mixing bowl, together with the cornflour and baking powder. Add the vegetable oil and stir in enough water to make a thick, smooth batter (about 175 ml/6 fl oz).

2 Pour the vegetable oil for deep-frying into a preheated wok or large frying pan and heat until almost smoking.

3 Dip the pork cubes into the batter and deep fry, in batches, until cooked through. Remove from the wok with a slotted spoon and drain on kitchen paper. Set aside and keep warm.

4 Drain all but 1 tablespoon of oil from the wok and return it to the heat. Add the onion, pepper, pineapple, carrot and bamboo shoots and stir-fry for 1–2 minutes. Remove from the wok with a slotted spoon and set aside.

5 Mix the sauce ingredients together and pour into the wok. Bring to the boil, stirring until thickened and clear. Cook for 1 minute, then return the pork and vegetables to the wok. Cook for a further 1–2 minutes, then transfer to a serving plate and serve with rice or noodles.

SZECHUAN WHITE FISH

>Serves 4 >Preparation time: 5 minutes >Cooking time: 20 minutes

INGREDIENTS

350 g/12 oz white fish fillets

1 small egg, beaten

25 g/1 oz plain flour

4 tbsp dry white wine

3 tbsp light soy sauce

vegetable oil, for frying

1 garlic clove, cut into slivers

1 tsp finely chopped fresh root ginger

1 onion, finely chopped

1 celery stick, chopped

1 red chilli, chopped

3 spring onions, chopped

1 tsp rice wine vinegar

$\frac{1}{2}$ tsp ground Szechuan pepper

175 ml/6 fl oz fish stock

1 tsp caster sugar

1 tsp cornflour

2 tsp water

METHOD

1 Cut the fish into 4-cm/1½-inch cubes. Beat together the egg, flour, wine and 1 tablespoon of soy sauce to make a batter. Dip the cubes of fish into the batter to coat well.

2 Heat the oil in a wok or large frying pan, reduce the heat slightly and cook the fish, in batches, for 2–3 minutes, until golden brown. Remove with a slotted spoon, drain on kitchen paper, set aside and keep warm.

3 Pour all but 1 tablespoon of oil from the wok and return to the heat. Add the garlic, ginger, onion, celery, chilli and spring onions and stir-fry for 1–2 minutes. Stir in the remaining soy sauce and the vinegar.

4 Add the Szechuan pepper, fish stock and caster sugar to the wok. Mix the cornflour with the water to form a smooth paste and stir it into the stock. Bring to the boil and cook, stirring, for 1 minute, until the sauce thickens and clears.

5 Return the fish cubes to the wok and cook for 1–2 minutes. Serve hot.

SWEET & SOUR VEGETABLES & TOFU

>Serves 4 >Preparation time: 5 minutes >Cooking time: 15 minutes

INGREDIENTS

1 tbsp groundnut oil

2 garlic cloves, crushed

1 tsp grated fresh root ginger

50 g/1¼ oz baby corn cobs

50 g/1¼ oz mangetouts

1 carrot, cut into matchsticks

1 green pepper, cut into matchsticks

8 spring onions, trimmed

50 g/1¼ oz canned bamboo shoots

225 g/8 oz marinated firm tofu, cubed

2 tbsp dry sherry

2 tbsp rice vinegar

2 tbsp clear honey

1 tbsp light soy sauce

150 ml/5 fl oz vegetable stock

1 tbsp cornflour

METHOD

1 Heat the groundnut oil in a preheated wok or large frying pan until almost smoking.

2 Add the garlic and grated root ginger and cook for 30 seconds, stirring frequently.

3 Add the baby corn cobs, mangetouts, carrot and pepper and stir-fry for about 5 minutes or until the vegetables are tender.

4 Add the spring onions, bamboo shoots and tofu and cook for a further 2 minutes.

5 Stir in the sherry, rice vinegar, honey, soy sauce, vegetable stock and cornflour and bring the mixture to the boil. Reduce the heat and simmer for 2 minutes. Transfer to serving dishes and serve hot.